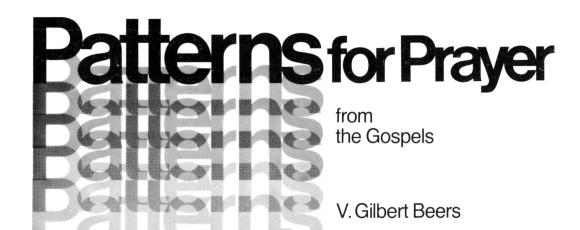

Patterns for Prayer

from
the Gospels

V. Gilbert Beers

Fleming H. Revell Company
Old Tappan, New Jersey

Scripture quotations in this volume are from *The King James Version of the Bible.*

Library of Congress Cataloging in Publication Data

Beers, Victor Gilbert, date
Patterns for prayer from the Gospels.

    1. Bible. N.T. Gospels—Prayers. I. Title
BV228.B4   226'.*6   72-3909
ISBN 0-8007-0545-9

What's In This Book

A prayer for those who wait

Simeon's Prayer

Luke 2: 25-33

Pathway to prayer

What led to Simeon's prayer

Forty days had passed since Jesus was born in Bethlehem. The sounds of the angel choir had long since faded from the skies. The shepherds had returned to the lonely hillsides to guard their sheep and wonder at the things they had seen and heard.

The manger where the Child had been born belonged to the animals once more. Mary and Joseph had moved Him into a home, joining the sleepy life-style of the little village.

On the eighth day, they had circumcised Him and given Him the name Jesus, as the Angel Gabriel had commanded. Now, after the forty-day wait, they made their way to Jerusalem to obey another command.

Already Mary and Joseph had obeyed God and let His Son adopt them as a family on earth. Already they had obeyed Caesar and put their names on his tax rolls. Already they had obeyed the Angel Gabriel and named the child Jesus.

In Jerusalem, they would make their way to the Temple so they could obey the Law of Moses. The Law required that they observe two ceremonies. First, Mary and Joseph must give the Child to a priest as a symbolic act of giving the firstborn child to the Lord. The priest would pray, then return the Child to the parents. They would "redeem" Him by paying about twenty-days' wages to the priest.

When that ceremony ended, Mary and Joseph would purchase two doves and give them to a priest. This priest would offer the doves at the altar as a purification for Mary.

But when Mary and Joseph came into the Temple, something strange happened to them. Before they could begin either ceremony, they were met by an old man named Simeon.

Simeon had waited, perhaps for many years, for a special Child to be brought to the Temple. He did not know the name of this Child or His family. But he knew that the Child would be God's Son, the Messiah for whom people had waited so long.

Simeon's last years had been hanging by a single divine thread of promise. The Holy Spirit had promised the old man that he would not die until he had seen the Messiah. That day had come at last and Simeon hurried to the Temple to see this special Baby.

The old man Simeon must have trembled as he lifted the Baby Jesus into his arms. God had given him the Good News that this was the Saviour, the One who would become King of kings and Lord of lords.

Out of the overflow of joy, Simeon began to praise God. Then he prayed this prayer to the Lord who had let him wait and see what men had longed to see for many years.

Simeon's Prayer

Luke 2:29-32

> Lord, now lettest thou thy servant depart
> in peace, according to thy word:
> For mine eyes have seen thy salvation,
> Which thou hast prepared before the
> face of all people;
> A light to lighten the Gentiles, and the
> glory of thy people Israel.

Patterns for prayer

from Simeon's prayer

Waiting is forever—or so it seems.

When we wait, eternity seems to replace the calendar or clock. Minutes of intense clock-watching can seem like days. Ten hours of delight pass more quickly than ten minutes of waiting.

Waiting wears our patience thin. The most calm, collected person becomes easily frustrated through waiting. Nerves stretch tight like rubber bands, ready to snap out at someone else or back at us.

Waiting is the calm at the eye of a storm. While the world rushes madly around us, we freeze into a point of time and space. Inside, all systems are on go, but we can't go because something we wait for has grounded us.

Waiting is a husband in a dress shop while his wife tries on dresses. It is a child counting the days until Christmas, or his birthday, or the end of school.

Waiting is a wife, with dinner ready and a husband who is late. It is anyone in a doctor's waiting room, counting the number who are still ahead of him.

People who wait are often watchmen. They stand guard against eventualities—harmful or beneficial. This may be the birth of a new baby, graduation from school, the visit of someone important, or a promotion. Waiting is standing by at the hospital, or airport, or train station. It is watching the mail for some important letter or package to come. Sometimes waiting is watching for something we believe the Lord is about to do in our lives.

Like a guard in ancient watchtowers, we stand alert to the coming of these events into our lives. And while we wait, we strain inwardly, hoping for time to pass more quickly and relieve the tension of our job as a watchman.

Simeon was a watchman, waiting for the Messiah to come so he could announce His coming to those nearby. Like all watchmen, Simeon must have recognized the plight, and delight, of his task. Like all watchmen, Simeon faced hours of waiting for moments of service.

The Bible does not say how long Simeon waited. We may suspect that it was a wait of many years, perhaps half a lifetime, far more than we are usually called upon to wait.

Waiting is anticipation. It is worry. It is fear. It is high expectations. It is apprehension. It is any one of many reactions to the unknown results of our waiting.

How we wait makes a great difference in what we become while waiting. What we do during our waiting, whom we seek for companionship and help, and our own attitudes and prayers—these all shape our lives and leave us frustrated or rewarded.

There are great lessons to be learned from the old man Simeon, who waited for the Saviour. In his prayer, we may find patterns to help us in our prayers while we wait for life to mature.

PATTERN FOR PRAYER
We Wait More Certainly When
We Invite God to Wait With Us

There is a strange fabric woven into our lives as we wait
for something. The threads of hope and despair mingle together
in crazy quilt fashion, leaving us puzzled as to which will
dominate the final design.

The fact that we wait for something suggests that we still
have hope. When all hope ends, so does our waiting.

Thus, if we wait at all, we admit to ourselves and the
world that we are waiting for something. And we admit also
that we hope for that for which we wait.

Some waiting brings great pleasure, for we build dream
castles that stagger our sense of reality. The day before
Christmas is a pleasant time of waiting for a child, for it
is a day of dreams and high hopes. There are some who say the
anticipation is even more pleasant than the reality of the
event for which we wait.

Unfortunately our waiting is not always that happy. Sometimes we begin to see more threads of despair than threads of
hope. The child waits happily the day before Christmas because
he is assured of a happy conclusion to come soon. But it is
unusual for us to know the final act in life's waiting drama
that clearly.

Most of our waiting is done with a painful uncertainty. Since we are not God, we cannot know tomorrow as we know yesterday. This gives us a sense of insecurity. Thus, if we wait alone, we can expect to be lonely as we wait. We can expect to be the sole heir of our own insecurity.

There is something about Simeon and his attitudes which speaks of security. The prayer of Simeon was not the prayer of a grumpy old man, soured on life. It was not the prayer of a bitter person, tired of waiting half a lifetime for a few minutes with a baby.

Simeon prayed with the optimism of youth, even though he spoke of dying. He blessed God (v. 28) and spoke of hope for all people (vs. 30, 31). His words caused Joseph and Mary to marvel or wonder (v. 33).

There is an easy answer for Simeon's optimism and confidence. While he had been "waiting for the consolation of Israel," "the Holy Ghost was upon him" (v. 25).

The story of Simeon suggests a wait of many years. But there is no suggestion of impatience or despair in his waiting. The Spirit of God had given him the assurance that he would not die until he had seen the Messiah, the Son of God. But even so, it is hard to wait so long for something so important.

Simeon must have looked forward each morning to the hope

of God's promise coming true that day. But if he did, there
must have been a temptation to be disappointed each evening
when nothing had happened.

When God waits with us, He helps us see more clearly through
His long-range vision. We are creatures of the moment, expect-
ing answers and actions now. God is the Creator of eternity,
not subject to hurry or frustration. If we really pray for
God to wait with us, we must be prepared to adjust to His
companionship and His perspective.

The presence of God makes us more secure as it strengthens
our patience. You know how time drags when you wait alone.
You know also how impatient you get when the moments tick by
one by one. But how much your patience is strengthened when
a friend waits with you. If the Holy Spirit waits with you,
He will strengthen you and your patience more than many other
friends.

A lonely wait often ends in bitterness and frustration.
Day after day after day we wait without an answer. Month after
month, or year after year, we wait with a growing uncertainty.
Hope dims, eclipsed by despair. There is no one to comfort.
No one to sit with us in the waiting room of life and remind
us of the glory of tomorrow. The lonely wait is too much for
us and we give up inside.

That's why it is so important to have God's Spirit with
us as we wait. Like Simeon, we can come to the end of our

long wait with praise on our lips (v. 28) and a testimony to
God's great hope (vs. 30-32).

PATTERN FOR PRAYER
We Wait With More Confidence When
We Claim God's Promises

If a good friend of yours said, "Tomorrow I'll bring over
a gift I bought for you on my trip," would you fret and worry
about getting the gift? Not unless you are neurotic or your
friend is dishonest.

When a good friend makes a promise like that, we accept
it as though the gift were already in our hands. We are confident that our friend's actions are as valid as his word.

If we feel that way about a good friend, how much more
should we feel that way about our God, "for he is faithful
that promised" (Hebrews 10: 23). If imperfect friends can
generate confidence in us, shouldn't a perfect God do even
more?

Through Simeon's time of waiting, he clung to a promise.
"And it was revealed unto him by the Holy Ghost, that he
should not see death, before he had seen the Lord's Christ"
(Luke 2:26). God had promised Simeon that he would see the
Messiah, God's Son, before he died. Since Simeon was "just
and devout" (v. 25), he took God at His word.

It's easy to believe God's promises when we realize who God is. Would the Creator of all the earth, the perfect Ruler of all heaven, lie to you? Would the Father of our Lord and Saviour, Jesus Christ, back out of a promise? No, what God promises, He will perform. What He says, He will do.

When we are confident that God has really promised something, we can be confident in waiting for it. When we sincerely believe that God wants us to have something, we can sincerely trust Him to give it to us.

Perhaps you have waited for something for many months, or years. You've wondered, down deep in your heart, if this for which you wait will ever happen.

Is what you wait for in harmony with the promises of God? After searching the promises and character of God, is it something you sincerely believe He wants you to have? Have you earnestly prayed for God's will to be done, and not your own?

Remember Simeon! Wait and pray in confidence by claiming the promises of God. Then, like Simeon, you will be led by the Holy Spirit of God into the answer to your prayers (v. 27).

PATTERN FOR PRAYER
God's Blessings to Us
Deserve Our Blessing to God

"Then took he him [Simeon took the Baby Jesus] up in his arms, and blessed God" (v. 28).

We don't often read about men blessing God, even though the Bible is filled with talk about God blessing men. How can men bless God?

Some translators use the words *praised God* here. That may help us to understand a little more what Simeon did.

But the words are not as essential as the deed. As Simeon lifted the Infant Messiah into his arms, after so many years of waiting, it was only natural for him to lift his heart to God, the Father of this Baby.

It was God who had brought Simeon through the long night of waiting into this glorious moment. God had blessed Simeon greatly through this experience. Now it was only right and fair that Simeon should return some of that blessing to God.

You must know of a hundred ways in which God has blessed you, or shown His favor to you. But can you think of one way you have blessed Him, or shown your favor to Him?

Let's think of a few. We bless God with our praise, as Simeon did. We bless Him with our conduct, as the "just and devout" Simeon did (v. 25). We bless Him with our testimonies, our songs, our quiet times alone with Him, our Christian influence, our witnessing, our prayers, and so many, many more.

If God has blessed you, try blessing Him in return. Remember Simeon!

PATTERN FOR PRAYER
Prayer Is the Proper Conclusion to a Successful Time of Waiting

Have you waited for something and it finally happened? What did you do then? Did you do what Simeon did? Simeon prayed . He gave praise to God. He testified to Jesus as the Son of God. He spoke great words of hope in his prayer.

So many people know instinctively what to do when they fail. They complain bitterly. Or, they cry out to God and ask His help. We should know as instinctively what to do when we succeed, when our waiting has turned out all right, after all. We should cry out to God and praise Him.

When we begin a project, we should talk to God about help. When we successfully conclude a project we should talk to God about our gratitude and praise.

Simeon had completed his long wait as a watchman for God. He had seen Jesus and had witnessed to others that this was God's Son. His work was over. So Simeon prayed that God would graduate him into his eternal rest. We may not be ready for that yet, but we should pray that God will graduate us into a new and greater responsibility.

When you begin a new work, pray! When you perform that new work, pray! When you wait for long intermissions, pray! When you successfully conclude your wait and your work, pray! There is really nothing more important that you could do.

Prayer reminders

When you pray and wait, remember to:

Pray that God will wait with you, to be a constant companion.

Pray that God will give you patience to wait on and on without giving up.

Pray that God will give you comfort and assurance to keep on hoping for that which you believe He wants you to have.

Pray that God will give you wisdom and counsel to make the right choices and decisions concerning your waiting.

Pray that God will help you wait for the right things, those which He wants you to have.

Pray that God will send friends to wait with you and be of help to you.

Pray that God will send you to friends who need your help while they wait.

Pray that you will give honor to God and His Son Jesus when your wait is over and God gives you a reward.

Pray that you will remain faithful to God and His trust in you when the wait grows long and tedious.

A prayer for those who follow Jesus

The Lord's Prayer

Matthew 6: 9-13
(Also Luke 11: 1-4)

Pathway to prayer

What led to The Lord's Prayer

Wherever Jesus went throughout Galilee, crowds gathered around Him. Some people came to be healed, or to bring a friend or relative for healing. Others wanted to hear Him preach and teach. Many came because they were curious.

The crowds came from everywhere. Some were from Galilee, others from Jerusalem and Judea, and some came from the other side of the Jordan River (Matthew 4: 25). Many people came to Jesus long enough to get what they wanted, and then they were gone. But some would not leave Him. They followed Him everywhere He went. These people became known as Jesus' disciples.

There were times when Jesus went somewhere to be alone with His disciples. He wanted to teach them about God and heaven and the way His followers should live here on earth. The crowds were not ready to hear all He had to say. Some would not understand what He said. Others hated Him because He did not follow the complex rules of the Pharisees.

One day Jesus left the crowds that had gathered from all parts of the country. He went with His disciples into a mountain where they could be alone. Then He sat down and taught them (5: 1, 2).

What Jesus said to His disciples that day has been called
The Sermon on the Mount. It could have been called The Lesson
on the Mount, for Jesus taught many important truths in it.
This sermon, or lesson, is found in Matthew 5, 6, and 7.

One of the important parts of The Sermon on the Mount is
a model prayer which Jesus gave to His disciples. That prayer
is known as The Lord's Prayer because our Lord Himself com-
posed it. This prayer is still a pattern for prayer to those
of us who follow Jesus Christ today.

The Lord's Prayer

Matthew 6:9-13

After this manner therefore pray ye: Our Father which art in heaven, Hallowed be thy name.

Thy kingdom come. Thy will be done in earth, as it is in heaven.

Give us this day our daily bread.

And forgive us our debts, as we forgive our debtors.

And lead us not into temptation, but deliver us from evil:

For thine is the kingdom, and the power, and the glory, for ever. Amen.

Patterns for prayer

from The Lord's Prayer

"After this manner therefore pray ye."

How do we know the way we should pray? Jesus said to pattern your prayers after this one.

How do we know how we should live as Christians? Pattern our lives after His. That is part of the idea of following Jesus.

Those who follow Jesus are called disciples. There were disciples who followed Him while He was on earth. And there are disciples who follow Him today.

What does it mean to follow Jesus?

Jesus said, "Whosoever will come after me, let him deny himself, and take up his cross, and follow me" (Mark 8: 34). Paul said, "As ye have therefore received Christ Jesus the Lord, so walk ye in him" (Colossians 2: 6).

Christians are people who have given their lives to Christ so that He can pattern them after His life. When sins are forgiven, we step out into a new life in Christ.

How shall we live that new life? What shall we do as Christians?

Be like Jesus. Follow in His steps. Live as His disciples. Pattern your life after His.

But how do we know enough of His life to follow? It's there in the Bible. That is why it is so important to read and understand the Bible. It teaches us how to become a Christian, then how to live as a Christian, or follower of Christ. That is why it is so important to seek the help and counsel of those who have studied much in God's Word.

"After this manner pray ye."

After this manner live ye.

If you want to follow Jesus, if you want to pattern your prayers after His, try to understand what He did and said. Then you will live and pray "after this manner." You will live and pray in His steps.

PATTERN FOR PRAYER
We Should Pray to a Loving
Father in Heaven

"Our Father which art in heaven." The words come easily, but it takes a while longer to reflect on their full meaning.

The ancient pagans did not acknowledge the existence of a loving God. So, they never had a personal relationship with Him.

Many people are like that today. Some will even admit that there is someone called God, but they do not know Him as a God of love. So they do not know Him in a personal relationship.

Christians know God through His Son, Jesus Christ. They know Him because they believed Him when He said that He "so loved the world that He gave his only begotten Son" (John 3:16). They know Him because they responded to His love in His Son.

We who are Christians have a great privilege that the Old Testament men and women did not have. It was not until Jesus came that men could call God "our Father." Jesus told us to do it. "After this manner therefore pray ye: Our Father which art in heaven."

What is a father? If you have had a happy relationship

with your earthly father, you will understand the meaning of "Our Father which art in heaven" a little better. If you have not, you will need to search longer for a proper understanding.

A father is someone instrumental in the creation of his child. Your father had a vital part in your origin. He also took care of you, giving you the essentials to proper growth. And while you grew, he gave you leadership and companionship. But most important, he gave you love—a certain kind of love that no other man could bestow upon you.

So it is with our Father in heaven, but even more so. Our Father in heaven was not only instrumental in our creation, He was the source of our life. He not only gives us the essentials to proper growth, He is the source of those essentials. He offers a certain kind of love that only He can give.

With the privilege of calling God our Father comes the responsibility of living as His children. First, it requires that we really have become a child of God, born again (John 3: 7) into His family. It requires also that we bring honor to our Father and keep our relationship as child and Father in proper perspective.

When we pray "Our Father" we enter into the presence of Someone who loves us as an earthly father loves his child. We tell Him our needs and ask for His help as an earthly child does with his father. And we expect our Father to respond, as a child expects his father to supply his needs.

PATTERN FOR PRAYER
We Should Pray to
Honor Our Father's Name

Have you ever asked yourself why you pray? Is it to bring God to the rescue, to bail you out of trouble? Or is it to ask God to play Santa Claus to you? Do you really have a more valid motive?

Jesus gave a better motive in His model prayer. "Hallowed be thy name." Christians should pray to honor God's name.

Children have a responsibility to honor their family name. Through their behavior, their attitudes, the words they speak, and the honors they gain, they add to the good name of their family.

But children who live mean and selfish lives dishonor their family name. Children of the Heavenly Father dishonor Him through words and deeds that are selfish. If we pray only to get ourselves out of trouble, we make prayer a selfish act. If we pray only to ask God for more things, we again make prayer a selfish act.

In the Garden of Gethsemane, Jesus told His Father how much He wanted to be freed from the responsibility of dying for all men. But then He prayed for God's will, not His, to be done (Matthew 26: 39). It was a prayer to honor His Father in heaven.

Are you tempted to pray earnestly for something because
you want it, even though you are not sure that God wants you
to have it? Are you tempted to pray for something you know
will bring dishonor to you as a Christian and therefore to
God? Are you tempted to pray for something that will glorify
you, but not God? Honor your Father's name when you pray. Pray
for those things you know will be in harmony with His will.

PATTERN FOR PRAYER
We Should Pray to Bring
Heaven Into Earth's Affairs

Jesus said we should pray like this, "Thy kingdom come. Thy
will be done in earth, as it is in heaven."

But have you ever thought about the way God will answer
this prayer? Have you realized that God may answer it through
you?

When you ask God to send His kingdom into earth, prepare
yourself to be His messenger. Be ready to serve as His ambassador, winning subjects to your King by representing Him
well. "Thy kingdom come—through me!"

When you pray for God's will to be done in earth, have you
thought about the way that would be answered? Have you seen

yourself seeking earnestly to do God's will in all you do?
Have you seen yourself patterning your earthly conduct after
your Heavenly Father's will? "Thy will be done—through me!"

The earth certainly needs a change, doesn't it? Our con-
temporary society needs help. Every Christian probably agrees
that we should pray for our neighborhood, our community, our
city, or state, our nation, and our world. But many Christians
are not sure about the way God will answer that prayer. How
will God's kingdom come, and God's will be done in earth?
Through me and you!

Jesus had already told His disciples that before He told
them how to pray. "Ye are the salt of the earth," He said.
"Ye are the light of the world" (Matthew 5: 13, 14). If the
world is to be changed, it is through the messengers of Christ.

Do you ever pray, "Help me bring thy light to the world,
Lord?" Do you ever ask God to use you as His salt to change
the insipid life around you?

The prayer of the Christian should be a prayer of personal
involvement. "Thy kingdom come. Thy will be done in earth,
as it is in heaven—through me!"

PATTERN FOR PRAYER
*We Should Pray to Involve
God in Our Breadwinning*

The job of breadwinning has changed much since Jesus gave
The Lord's Prayer. Jesus' contemporaries were concerned mostly
about earning a daily wage for food, clothing, and shelter.

Today we have almost buried ourselves in the complex job
of earning and spending money. The treasury, taxes, and tax
collectors go back to the time of Christ and beyond. But such
terms as bonds, stocks, brokers, securities, pensions, insurance
plans, policies, consumers, franchises, trusts, and others
were not part of breadwinning then.

Spending our money is almost more complex today than earning it. But earning it can be very frustrating and demanding.
Against the backdrop of tax forms and business record keeping,
the simple phrase, "Give us this day our daily bread" seems
almost too simple.

Yet the simplicity of this statement takes us back to the
basics of daily needs. The intricacies of modern finance are
a man-made monster, brought into being to police another man-
made monster—materialism and its appetites. The word *needs*
is broadened today to include luxuries that would stagger the
mind of a Bible-time king. Solomon would have given half his

kingdom for the gadgets we have in our homes. But we still call them needs.

Thus, when we pray "Give us this day our daily bread," we don't think of the simple bread of Jesus' day. We let our minds slide a bit on the word *bread* until it swallows up half the Sears catalog, some life insurance policies, a few stocks, a savings account, and a new car.

Are we really praying for daily bread, or are we praying for God to help us keep up with the Joneses? Only you can answer that question for yourself.

As we run the risk of praying for too much in our bread-winning, we sometimes run the risk of praying for too little. To pray for too much is to lack discretion. To pray for too little is to lack faith.

Jesus' model prayer suggests the proper balance. "Give us this day our *daily* bread." It is proper to ask God for the true necessities of life, enough for the day but not more. It was the balance which God gave to the Israelites when they asked for bread and He sent manna—enough for each day but no more.

Perhaps we can each examine our own prayers for bread. We certainly want to pray up to our faith level, but not beyond our discretion level.

PATTERN FOR PRAYER
We Should Pray to
Ask God's Forgiveness

There is a rather sobering little word with only two letters in this part of Jesus' prayer. It is the word *as.*

This word suggests that we may ask for God's forgiveness for our sins if we have first offered our forgiveness to those who have sinned against us. If so, we are forced to examine our own attitude of forgiveness. Do we still hold a grudge against someone? Have we forgiven someone but not forgotten? If so, we really haven't forgiven at all, for that implies forgetting.

Jesus was saying that we ought not go to God to ask forgiveness until we have first made things right with others. Jesus had already said this in The Sermon on the Mount, perhaps no more than five minutes before The Lord's Prayer was given. "Therefore if thou bring thy gift to the altar, and there rememberest that thy brother hath ought against thee; Leave there thy gift before the altar, and go thy way; first be reconciled to thy brother, and then come and offer thy gift" (Matthew 5: 23, 24).

On another occasion, Jesus told a parable of a king's servant who owed ten million dollars. When he begged the king for mercy, the king forgave his debt. But when a fellow servant begged this man for mercy, he would not forgive his fellow servant's twenty-dollar debt.

When the king learned what had happened, he was very angry and "delivered him to the tormentors" (18:34). Then Jesus ended His parable by saying, "So likewise shall my heavenly Father do also unto you, if ye from your hearts forgive not every one his brother their trespasses" (v. 35).

So Jesus took very seriously this matter of forgiving one another. He associated it closely with our request for God's forgiveness.

This does not mean that we should avoid seeking God's forgiveness. It means that, before we do, we must forgive others who have wronged us.

When you pray, ask God to forgive. But when you ask God to forgive, be sure you pray from a forgiving heart.

PATTERN FOR PRAYER
We Should Pray for God's Help in Facing Temptation

"Lead us not into temptation." At first glance, this is a puzzling statement. James 1: 13 clearly says, "Let no man say when he is tempted, I am tempted of God: for God cannot be tempted with evil, neither tempteth he any man."

So Jesus was not suggesting that God would ever cause us to be tempted or lead us into temptation. But what was He saying?

The meaning is clearer when we move the punctuation marks. "Lead us, not into temptation, but deliver us from evil." Or, to put it into other words, "Lead us away from temptation, spare us from evil."

In the Garden of Gethsemane, Jesus told His disciples, "Pray that ye enter not into temptation" (Luke 22: 40). Again He warned them, "Watch and pray, lest ye enter into temptation" (Mark 14: 38). We are the ones who walk into temptation. He is the one who can warn us about the danger of our way. He is the one who can divert our paths away from evil.

Only God knows the future. There are people who guess some future events, and do it with some degree of accuracy. But God alone knows everything that will happen in your life today, and tomorrow, and all the days until you make your final earthly appointment with God.

Since God knows all about us and our future, He knows the risks we will take and the dangers we will encounter and the temptations we will face. He knows that place where you could yield to temptation and fall.

That is why it is so important to pray often, "Lead us away from temptation, spare us from evil."

The fact that all of us occasionally yield to temptations suggests that all of us need help to keep from yielding. But who is strong enough, and wise enough, and kind enough to give us that help? Try God!

PATTERN FOR PRAYER
We Should Pray to Bring Honor and Glory to God

"For thine is the kingdom, and the power, and the glory, for ever. Amen."

As the chief purpose of man is to honor and glorify God, so is the chief purpose of man's prayers. "Glorify God in your body, and in your spirit, which are God's" (1 Corinthians 6: 20).

If we constantly weigh our prayers to see if the answers would bring honor and glory to God, we will understand about our need to pray. We pray, not because we must escape from something, or because we want to have something, but because we want to enter into something—a vital relationship with God that will bring honor and glory to Him.

Prayer reminders

When you pray as you follow Jesus, remember to:

Pray as you would talk to a father, someone who loves you very much and wants the best for you.

Pray as an obedient child, remembering your responsibility to conduct yourself so that you will honor your Father.

Pray for those things which are in harmony with God's will, not merely things that you want to satisfy your own desires.

Pray that God will use you as His messenger to bring heaven into the affairs of earth.

Pray that God will do His work through you, using you to bring His influence into the world.

Pray that God will help you do your best in earning the necessities of life.

Pray for those who have sinned against you, that you may forgive them.

Pray for forgiveness for those things you have done against the Lord.

Pray that God will lead you away from temptation and will spare you from evil.

Pray that all you ask for and do will bring honor to God.

A prayer for people in trouble

Peter's Prayer

Matthew 14: 22-33

Pathway to prayer

What led to Peter's prayer

The crowd had seen a miracle! Jesus had fed more than five thousand people with only five loaves and two fishes. They realized that Jesus was more than an ordinary man. He had done something that no man could do.

The people must have talked much about this miracle as Jesus sent them back to their homes. When they were gone, Jesus told His disciples to go to the other side of the Sea of Galilee, where He would join them later.

As Jesus stayed behind to pray, His disciples set sail by night to cross over the sea. But before they could get to the other side, the winds blew against them and they were not able to make progress.

The small fishing boat must have bobbed about on the turbulent sea for many hours, going nowhere. Somewhere between three and six in the morning, the weary and frightened disciples looked out across the dark waves and saw a figure walking across the sea toward them. They did not know that it was Jesus.

The disciples cried out that it was a ghost. But Jesus heard their cry and spoke to them. "It is I; be not afraid," He said (Matthew 14:27).

Peter was overjoyed to find that it was Jesus and that He was walking on top of the stormy waves.

"Let me do it, too," Peter asked, almost childlike. When Jesus gave permission, Peter stepped from the boat and began walking to Jesus on the water.

But suddenly Peter realized what he was doing. Peter's childlike belief began to be replaced by adult reasoning. Then he became afraid. When he gained his reason, he lost his faith and began to sink.

As Peter began to slip hopelessly beneath the waves, he cried out a prayer of desperation. But it has become a prayer for all those who get into trouble.

Peter's Prayer

Matthew 14:30   *Lord, save me.*

Patterns for prayer

from Peter's prayer

Peter represents so many of us. He bit off more than he could chew and got into trouble. He ventured into something over his head before he realized the danger. When he got into the midst of his venture, Peter chickened out. But there was no turning back. He was in trouble and there seemed to be no hope.

Peter's situation, and ours, has many names. You may call it a crisis, a mess, a dilemma, an emergency, or a predicament. When some of us get into trouble, we say we're in a pickle or in hot water.

But whatever the name, Peter's problem and ours are similar. We dream with confidence, step out with uncertainty, and mire down in hopelessness.

Trouble comes in many forms. We say we're in trouble when we can't pay our bills, or when we leave the car window open as it goes through the car wash, or when we're dragged into court to answer charges.

Trouble is burning your bridges behind you, or cutting off the one person who can build bridges before you. It is destroying that which can help us most.

Trouble is starting to build before we count the cost. It is spending more than we make or eating more than we can digest or taking on more than we can finish. Sometimes it is trying to keep up with the Joneses.

Trouble is a sour marriage, a declining career, or a deteriorating personal life. Or it is all three combined.

Trouble is like a brick wall built across our path. It seems there's no way through it and such a long way around it. We fear our trouble lest it stop our progress. We are irritated because we wanted an easy way and trouble forces us to rethink the way we will go from here.

Many people talk of a mess in their lives. They have gotten themselves into trouble, or many troubles, and they don't know the way out. Many young people today are talking about the mess that they or their friends are in. Life is a disaster area. Problems litter their path and they don't know which way to go from here.

Trouble is like that. It makes us frustrated because we see all the roadblocks and stop signs and barricades, but we don't understand how to read the detour signs. So trouble gives us a sense of insecurity and uncertainty because we don't know what to do or where to go.

People in trouble grope for answers. When panic sets in they look anywhere, even in the wrong places. Sometimes they simply exchange one set of crises for another more troublesome set. They jump from the frying pan into the fire. They do rash and foolish things to cover up other rash and foolish things.

Trouble comes from bad judgment, rash behavior, planned folly, or a lack of faith. It gets us into disfavor with loved ones, the law, our neighbors, or our own conscience. Trouble is getting ourselves into something over our head, or getting others turned against us, or creating circumstances which are not tolerable.

You may have some kind of trouble. If so, you are probably aware of it. And you are wondering what to do about it.

What do you do with your troubles? How do you handle them when they come to harass you?

Do you search for some way to destroy your troubles—or to rise above them or detour around them?

Do you look for some way to lighten your burdens—or to strengthen yourself so they are not so heavy to bear?

Do you struggle and wrestle with problems that seem to get the best of you—or do you find a friend who can handle them better than you can?

When Peter got into trouble, he cried out to a Friend, "Lord, save me." Then the Lord lifted him up out of his trouble and brought peace into his life.

When you get into trouble, that same Friend is nearby. And the same cry can bring the same answer.

But do not be surprised if the Lord sends added strength to you to help you carry your trouble. Or He may give you clearer detour signs so that you may find your way above or around your trouble. Or He may go with you to fight your way through your troubles.

The Lord works in many wonderful ways. Expect Him to answer, but not always in the same way. Expect Him to help, but not always in the way you may anticipate. The Lord will see you safely to the other side of your trouble if you trust Him. But He may get you there in some unique way which you do not expect.

PATTERN FOR PRAYER
Our Trouble May Wake Us Up
to Our Need to Pray

Some people are in trouble, but don't know it. Unfortunately, they sometimes do not wake up until it is too late.

Fear is sometimes a negative influence in our lives. We can be filled with fears and miss the joy of living. But, on the other hand, fear can be a friend to awaken us to serious trouble. Fear is a God-given guardian when it keeps us from ungodly pursuits. Fear should be a welcome guest when it prevents us from falling prey to danger.

Peter was afraid in his crisis. We are not completely sure if his fear weakened his faith and started him sinking, or if it awakened his need for God as he was sinking. Perhaps it was some of each. Peter must have been more afraid sinking into the sea than he had been walking on the waves.

Peter was certainly aware of his crisis. As he began to sink, he cried out for help. It was not just an ordinary S O S. Peter's cry for help was a fervent prayer. "Lord, save me."

Sometimes it takes one crisis to wake us up to another. How many marital crises have been eased because of a parent-child crisis? Or how many crises within a home are resolved by some threat from outside the home?

We may need an economic crisis to wake us up to a crisis in our career. Or an emotional crisis to cause us to realize that we have a physical crisis.

Whether we are awakened by another crisis, or by fear, the new awareness we have of our trouble at hand should cause us to cry out for help. When we realize we are in deep trouble, and there is nothing more we can do, it is time to cry, "Lord, save me."

These three words have changed the course of millions of lives, awakened to their need for eternal help beyond their own. People have awakened to the fact that they are sinking into an eternal sea of hopelessness, and the only hope is the Saviour who stands nearby.

"Lord, save me," they have cried. And the Lord saved them from the tempest of sin that raged in their lives. Perhaps you want to be saved that way, too. Like Peter, you should cry out, "Lord, save me." He's the only one who can really do it.

The presence of sin in our lives presents a never ending crisis. Unforgiven sin is a millstone around our necks. Our eternal destinies depend on God's forgiveness of sin. This is accomplished through the same Lord who walked on the waves with Peter. Because of His sacrifice at Calvary, He can answer the prayer that you pray, "Lord, save me."

PATTERN FOR PRAYER
The Lord Is Our Only Sure Hope in the Time of Trouble

The Lord to whom Peter prayed was the same Lord who "stretched forth his hand, and caught him [Peter]" (Matthew 14: 31). He was also the same Lord who scolded Peter for letting his lack of faith get him into trouble.

But however Peter got into trouble, it was the Lord who got him out. It was the same Lord who raised dead men from the grave and sick men from their cots.

Don't spend all your time analyzing your trouble and how you got into it. If Peter had done that, he would have gone to the bottom of the Sea of Galilee. How you got into trouble is history. That is not nearly so important as what you do with your trouble.

Do you want a postmortem on your trouble, or do you want out of it? Do you want to worry about your trouble, or do you want to let the Lord save you from it?

The final answer to life's greatest problems is the Lord. People who know, say that the only satisfactory answer to hard drug addiction is Jesus Christ—the same Christ who walked with Peter on the sea that night. Just as He was Peter's only hope, so is He the drug addict's only hope.

There are many things in life too complicated for us to handle by ourselves. There are many situations which are too involved. There are many problems too complex. But the Lord who knows all can answer life's deepest need.

Salvation in Jesus Christ is the ultimate answer to man's greatest problem—sin. Until we cry out with Peter's words, "Lord, save me," we are still at the mercy of our sin. Sin drags us down as surely as the waves of the sea dragged Peter under.

When we wake up to our eternal danger and cry out, we reach for our only sure hope. "Jesus stretched forth his hand, and caught him." That's still true today. It is Jesus who reaches out in mercy and catches us before we are lost forever.

No matter what your crisis is—money, marriage, job, or sin

dragging you under—your answer is the same. Call on Jesus Christ. "Lord, save me!" He will do the same for you that He did for Peter—stretch forth His hand and catch you and keep you from sinking into utter hopelessness.

PATTERN FOR PRAYER
The Lord Brings Peace When
He Removes Our Trouble

"And when they were come into the ship, the wind ceased. Then they that were in the ship came and worshiped him, saying, Of a truth thou art the Son of God" (Matthew 14: 32, 33).

There is something so right about that conclusion to the story of Peter. A calm came upon the scene, bringing a setting of peace. In that time of peace, there was worship. And the worship centered on the Christ, the Son of God, the Messiah, the King of kings, and Lord of the troubled heart.

That seems to be the proper postlude to a resolved crisis. The Lord brings salvation and peace. You bring a heart filled with worship for God's Son.

"Peace I leave with you, my peace I give unto you: not as the world giveth, give I unto you. Let not your heart be troubled, neither let it be afraid" (John 14: 27). Those were

Jesus' words to His disciples. They are for present-day disciples as well.

No crisis or trouble is too great but that the Prince of Peace can lift men from it and restore peace once more. That's because He is what the men in that fishing boat said he was—the Son of God.

Prayer reminders

When you are in trouble and pray, remember to:

Pray that God will give you help during your time of trouble.

Pray that God will give you stronger faith to meet your troubles, to make you strong enough to bear your burdens when He wants you to do this.

Pray in the spirit of worship and praise when the Lord helps you in the time of trouble.

Pray, even though the situation seems hopeless with no way out.

Pray that the Lord will save you from your trouble and from your sins.

Pray that the Lord will help you meet your trouble in His choice way.

A prayer for those who pray in public

The Pharisee's and the
Publican's Prayers

Luke 18: 9-14

Pathway to prayer

What led to the Pharisee's and
the publican's prayers

Jesus visited the Temple often, moving quietly among the crowds of people who came from all parts of Israel, and beyond. The Temple was the focal point of life in Israel. Men were required to come there three times each year to attend the important feasts. Of course, the women and children often came with them.

To any observant person, the Temple always presented one surprise after another. The open courtyards, crowded with the rich and poor, merchants and beggars, and people of all backgrounds, provided a steady stream of interesting sights.

Although the Temple was God's house, it had become a haven for dishonest merchants and moneychangers. The poor who came to buy pigeons and doves and sheep for sacrifices often found themselves cheated in their purchases. The worshiper who came to give or sacrifice often found himself shortchanged by the moneychangers.

While in the Temple one day, Jesus became angered by this dishonesty and threw over the moneychangers' tables and drove them from the Temple with a whip (John 2: 13-17). Later in His ministry, He would do this again (Matthew 21: 12, 13).

On another of His visits to the Temple, Jesus saw two men

who came to pray. Their prayers, and the way they approached their prayers made a strange incident. Later Jesus told some people a story about these two men.

The Bible calls this story a parable. It was something like a sermon illustration, or an anecdote to emphasize a lesson. It probably came from Jesus' visit to the Temple, although it is possible that Jesus made up the story. A parable did not have to be from real life.

Jesus' story was about a Pharisee and a publican. These two men were from radically different ways of life. The Pharisee was a proud, self-righteous religious leader who made life a rule book on strict behavior. The publican had put all personal pride aside to become a tax collector for the enemy, Rome. He was generally so dishonest that he honestly admitted it. He collected more taxes than he should and kept what he did not send on to the Romans.

Two men from two different worlds who came to pray. What would each have to say to God? What would a self-righteous religious leader and an openly dishonest tax collecter pray in the presence of each other?

What they prayed publicly in the Temple was so significant that Jesus used their story as a parable. Through this parable, we may each learn some important patterns for our own public prayers.

The Pharisee's and the Publican's Prayers

Luke 18:10-13

Two men went up into the temple to pray; the one a Pharisee, and the other a publican.

The Pharisee stood and prayed thus with himself, God, I thank thee, that I am not as other men are, extortioners, unjust, adulterers, or even as this publican.

I fast twice in the week, I give tithes of all that I possess.

And the publican, standing afar off, would not lift up so much as his eyes unto heaven, but smote upon his breast, saying, God be merciful to me a sinner.

Patterns for prayer

from the Pharisee's and
the publican's prayers

"Would you please lead us in prayer?"

"We will now be led in prayer by . . . ."

If these words strike terror in your heart, you are not alone. Many are afraid to pray in public and avoid it as much as possible.

"I can't say things as well as someone else."

"When I stand up and open my mouth, nothing wants to come out."

"What will other people around me think?"

"What if I don't say the right things?"

Too often, what should be an experience in worship becomes a hang-up. The thought of praying before others drives some of us to the back rows or completely out of the prayer service.

Dismayed, we remain silent in public services, reserving prayer for the quiet seclusion of home. We take comfort in Jesus' words, ". . . when thou prayest, enter into thy closet, and when thou hast shut thy door, pray to thy Father which is in secret. . ." (Matthew 6: 6).

Others may not face this same problem with public prayer. But it would not be surprising to find that most of us who pray in public are searching for some kind of help with our public prayers. Praying aloud before our friends and neighbors

is always a challenge, leaving us uncertain at times as to
what we should say.

The prayers of the Pharisee and publican, and the setting
in which they prayed, offer some interesting patterns for us
to consider as we think about public prayer. Here were two
men who prayed in public and Jesus heard them. What Jesus
said about their prayers can give us some understanding concerning our own public prayers.

PATTERN FOR PRAYER
We Should Pray in Public to Share
Our Needs, Not Our Righteousness

The Pharisee prayed to impress others with his goodness
and righteousness. The publican prayed to tell God about his
deficiencies.

The Pharisee impressed his neighbors with what he had. The
publican impressed God with what he needed.

The Pharisee made a long list of his plus qualities. The
publican simply told God about that one big minus in his life.

The Pharisee proudly shared his religious qualities. The
publican shamefully confessed his empty heart.

The Pharisee told God and his neighbors why he was just.
But the publican was the one who went home "justified rather
than the other."

The Pharisee told his neighbors and God why he was better than this sinner. But the publican simply confessed that he was a sinner.

The Pharisee stood up to pray "with himself." The publican would not "lift up so much as his eyes unto heaven, but smote upon his breast."

The Pharisee told much but asked for nothing. The publican had nothing to tell, but asked for much.

The Pharisee was proud. The publican was humble. The Pharisee was so pleased with his accomplishments that he did not realize that he needed help. The publican was so ashamed of his helplessness that he had nothing to be proud of.

Jesus said that the publican went home with his prayer answered. The Pharisee had no request, so there was no answer due. He already had his reward, his pride.

When we pray in public, we should remember the contrast between the Pharisee and the publican. We must not pray to display our goodness, but to share our needs.

We must realize that every person in the room with us has as many needs as we have. Every person is a sinner, just as we are, and the publican was, and the Pharisee also.

Some, like the Pharisee, may not realize how needy they are until we voice our own needs. But our prayer confesses our needs and strikes a harmonious chord in the minds and hearts of those about us. Our neighbors soon recognize that the needs we verbalize are their needs also.

Prayer must never elevate self. Prayer is the cry of a person who needs help, or the praise and thanks of a person who has received help.

We have so little goodness, that it isn't worth bragging about it. When the scales tip heavily on the side of our weaknesses, needs, and deficiencies, we should not spend the precious moments in God's presence reciting the small bit of goodness we have and leave our needs untouched.

We recognize easily that our private prayer time is the time to share our needs with God. But we have cultivated the idea that it is weak or embarrassing to share our needs in public.

Of course, there are very personal needs and problems which we do not share in public, lest we confuse our neighbors. But we should not hesitate to admit that we, like those about us, have many needs and that we pray for those needs privately and publicly.

PATTERN FOR PRAYER
We Should Pray in Public to Talk With God, Not Our Neighbors

This is a difficult truth for all of us to accept. For some strange reason, when we start to pray in public, we become more conscious of our neighbors than we are of God. We begin to say words for their benefit. We want all men to think well of us, and that includes the way we word our public prayers.

It is extremely difficult for any person to stand before others and promptly forget them. That goes against our human nature.

When the Pharisee began to pray, he obviously prayed for others to hear, even though he addressed himself to God to qualify his words as a prayer. Jesus said that the Pharisee was exalting himself through his prayer, trying to lift himself up before the eyes of his fellow men.

The Pharisee not only wanted men to think well of him, he wanted men to think more highly of him than of the publican. Through his prayer, the Pharisee was trying to sell his neighbors on his superiority. He knew that he couldn't sell God on this idea, so his prayer must have been directed to those around him.

If we pray to talk with God, then why do we need to pray in public at all? Why can't we go home and talk over our needs with God in private?

There is a time to pray in private and a time to pray in public. Our secret needs should be shared in secret. But there are needs we all share, and those can be verbalized in public.

If you are ready to confess personal sins, go into your own room to pray. If you are ready to express the needs or sins of a group, your prayer can represent the thoughts and confessions of those who hear you. You are verbalizing what all of your neighbors should be thinking about themselves.

The term "lead us in prayer" is probably the most correct in this sense. In public prayer, we give voice to the prayers that lie unexpressed in the hearts and minds of those who hear us.

Thus, if we merely recite our virtues, we sugarcoat the whole point of praying. But when we confess our collective sins, or bring collective needs to the Lord, we initiate a service of true worship.

It is true that some people are more skilled in verbalizing the needs and problems of us all. We should be grateful for those people, for they put our thoughts and desires into words which we might otherwise not know how to express.

But every one of us should be mature enough as a Christian to welcome the stumbling, halting prayer of a brother or sister in Christ who is honestly talking to God on our behalf. I would much rather hear that kind of prayer than the polished words of an eloquent person who has constructed a neat little sermon for his listeners.

The Pharisee had a neat little sermon for his neighbors. The publican had a crude little prayer for his God. But it was the publican who went home justified rather than the Pharisee.

Let us recognize that we can have eloquent prayers to God in our behalf and crude little sermons for our neighbors. We must not associate eloquence with pride or self-exaltation. Nor should we associate faltering speech with sincerity. Eloquence or incompetence have nothing to do with the content. That is simply the skill of the person who prays showing through. The point is very simply this—*what* we pray is more important than *how* we pray.

We all like to hear eloquent prayers which honestly express our needs and desires. We must be honest to admit we would rather hear those prayers than the faltering prayers which also express our needs and desires. But that should not keep the less eloquent person from praying, for we also want to hear him.

But when we sincerely want to worship, we do not appreciate the eloquent prayer, or faltering prayer, which is given to impress us instead of God. Let each of us pray to the best of our verbalizing skills, but let us be more concerned with bringing our needs and concerns, and those of our neighbors, to the Lord.

PATTERN FOR PRAYER
We Should Pray in Public
to Exalt God, Not Ourselves

When Jesus finished His story about the Pharisee and publican, He told the people something they should never forget.
Prayer is not to be used to exalt self. It is the opposite!
Prayer is an act of humility. Through prayer, we submit ourselves and our needs to God.

Jesus said, ". . . for every one that exalteth himself shall be
abased; and he that humbleth himself shall be exalted" (Luke 18: 14).
For that reason, Jesus said, "I tell you, this man [the pub-
lican] went down to his house justified rather than the
other [the Pharisee]" (v. 14).

Prayer is a means of putting ourselves in our proper
places. We should not destroy our personal worth, for in so
doing, we destroy our usefulness to God. But we should not
elevate ourselves beyond our actual worth, either, for in so
doing, we deceive ourselves. We begin to think we are self-
sufficient and that we do not need God. This was the Pharisee's
problem.

Pride distorts our image of personal worth. Pride turns us into a giant parade balloon, impressively big, but reduced to nothing by a mere pin prick. Pride pumps us up and hangs a thin cloak of self-sufficiency on us. Pride has nothing to support us but our own hot air. This does not make a very valid substance for prayer. Pride sent the Pharisee home empty-handed while the publican's humility sent him home justified.

Prayer reminders

When you pray in public, remember to:

Share your needs with the Lord instead of praying to impress your neighbors.

Pray with a greater consciousness of God than of your neighbors.

Pray to exalt God, not yourself.

Pray so that you express your neighbors' needs well, not so that you speak well.

Pray to the best of your ability to verbalize, but do not stop praying if you lack that skill.

Pray to put yourself in your proper place before God—not so low that you lose your usefulness, and not so high that you lose your sense of need for God.

A prayer for those who intercede

Jesus' Prayer of Intercession

John 17

Pathway to prayer

What led to Jesus' prayer

The day before Jesus' crucifixion was filled with many important events. During the afternoon, Peter and John had made arrangements for the evening meal in an upper room.

After sundown, Jesus and His disciples went to this upper room to eat The Last Supper together. There Jesus washed His disciples' feet, showing them that they were called to serve, not to rule. He ate the bread and drank the wine with them, establishing a service for Christians throughout the centuries to come.

While in the upper room, Jesus taught His disciples many truths, including the beautiful thoughts in John 14. At the end of this talk, Jesus said to them, "Arise, let us go hence" (John 14: 31). At that time Jesus and His disciples probably left the upper room.

Jesus had much more to teach His disciples before the night was over. The entire discourse in John 15 and 16, and the prayer in John 17 were given somewhere between the upper room and the eastern gate of the city.

John 18 begins with the words, "When Jesus had spoken these words, he went forth with his disciples over the brook Cedron, where there was a garden, into the which he entered, himself and his disciples." The teachings He gave, which are now John 15 and 16, and the prayer He prayed, now John 17, were given in the streets of Jerusalem or in the Temple.

Many believe that Jesus shared these teachings and the great prayer in John 17 with His disciples in their last visit together in God's House, the Temple. This seems more likely than the streets.

In the open courtyards of the Temple, with the moon and stars for a canopy above Him, Jesus had an appropriate setting for His discourse and prayer. What better place to talk *about* the Father than in His house? What better place to talk *to* the Father than in His house?

The prayer that Jesus gave in John 17 is a prayer of intercession, a Saviour praying for His disciples and others. In that prayer, Jesus gives us some patterns for our prayers as we intercede for others.

Jesus' Prayer of Intercession

John 17

These words spake Jesus, and lifted up his eyes to heaven, and said, Father, the hour is come; glorify thy Son, that thy Son also may glorify thee:

As thou hast given him power over all flesh, that he should give eternal life to as many as thou hast given him.

And this is life eternal, that they might know thee the only true God, and Jesus Christ, whom thou hast sent.

I have glorified thee on the earth; I have finished the work which thou gavest me to do.

And now, O Father, glorify thou me with thine own self with the glory which I had with thee before the world was.

I have manifested thy name unto the men which thou gavest me out of the world: thine they were, and thou gavest them me; and they have kept thy word.

Now they have known that all things whatsoever thou hast given me are of thee.

For I have given unto them the words which thou gavest me; and they have received them, and have known surely that I came out from thee, and they have believed that thou didst send me.

I pray for them: I pray not for the world, but for them which thou hast given me; for they are thine.

And all mine are thine, and thine are mine; and I am glorified in them.

And now I am no more in the world, but these are in the world, and I come to thee. Holy Father, keep through thine own name those whom thou hast given me, that they may be one, as we are.

While I was with them in the world, I kept them in thy name: those that thou gavest me I have kept, and none of them is lost, but the son of perdition; that the scripture might be fulfilled.

And now come I to thee; and these things I speak in the world, that they might have my joy fulfilled in themselves.

I have given them thy word; and the world hath hated them, because they are not of the world, even as I am not of the world.

I pray not that thou shouldest take them out of the world, but that thou shouldest keep them from the evil.

They are not of the world, even as I am not of the world.

Sanctify them through thy truth: thy word is truth.

As thou hast sent me into the world, even so have I also sent them into the world.

And for their sakes I sanctify myself, that they also might be sanctified through the truth.

Neither pray I for these alone, but for them also which shall believe on me through their word;

That they all may be one; as thou, Father, art in me, and I in thee, that they also may be one in us: that the world may believe that thou hast sent me.

And the glory which thou gavest me I have given them; that they may be one, even as we are one:

I in them, and thou in me, that they may be made perfect in one; and that the world may know that thou hast sent me, and hast loved them, as thou hast loved me.

Father, I will that they also, whom thou hast given me, be with me where I am; that they may behold my glory, which thou hast given me: for thou lovedst me before the foundation of the world.

O righteous Father, the world hath not known thee: but I have known thee, and these have known that thou hast sent me.

And I have declared unto them thy name, and will declare it; that the love wherewith thou hast loved me may be in them, and I in them.

Patterns for prayer

from Jesus' prayer
of intercession

Intercession—acting on behalf of two parties to reconcile differences.

To intercede is to bring people together. It is to make each person acceptable to the other. Intercession establishes friendships between those who have been apart.

The person who intercedes is a two-way bridge across a great gulf. He touches both sides which do not touch each other. He brings them into a vital relationship with one another.

Intercession is getting two quarrelsome children to say, "I'm sorry." It brings two church members with petty differences to the point where they can each say, "I was wrong."

Intercession is peacemaking—between equals or those who are not equal. It is an employee speaking to a boss on behalf of a fellow employee. It is a boss speaking to one employee on behalf of another. It is a public relations director speaking to the press on behalf of his client.

A person who intercedes cares for those he wants to bring together. His purpose is to help them both and encourage them to help one another. It is his hope that they will care for each other as he cares for both of them.

Intercession means giving up something. The one who intercedes gives up something to bring about reconciliation. Each person to be reconciled must give up something which keeps him apart from the other. Without personal sacrifice, or giving, there is no reconciliation.

But as all parties give, each one receives. Each who gave will get something better in return. All will be the richer.

Intercession is an effort to bring unity. The one who intercedes helps to bring the two parties into a oneness of thought and purpose.

What is intercession? It is negotiating an international settlement or helping to resolve a quarrel between two children. It is reconciling a husband and wife who have drifted apart or people of two races who have learned to hate each other.

Intercession is love, reaching out in opposite directions to touch two worlds and bring them together. It is peace, seeking a common ground for two points of view. It is joy, proving that reconciliation and unity and harmony do bring a lasting satisfaction.

But most of all, intercession is a loving Saviour, reaching one hand into the hand of His Heavenly Father, and the other into the hands of lost mankind. It is a Saviour who becomes a bridge between lost men and a loving God, reconciling them through Himself. It is Jesus, praying under the night stars on behalf of those He loves.

Intercession is also you, praying on behalf of another. It is you, asking for God's grace and mercy, not for yourself, but for someone else. In the prayer of Jesus, you will find patterns for your own prayers of intercession. Study His prayer, and you will discover how you ought to pray for others.

PATTERN FOR PRAYER
We Should Pray That God Will Help Us Bring Others to Him

"And this is life eternal, that they might know thee the only true God, and Jesus Christ, whom thou hast sent," Jesus prayed (John 17: 3).

This should be our prayer, too, that they might know Him. As Jesus is the bridge between us and God, so we also are the bridge between lost people and Jesus.

The work of interceding for those who do not know God is a sobering business. So much depends on us. How important it is to pray that God will give us all the wisdom and help we need to do this vital work.

We are interceding between a Saviour who has paid the full price to show His love and the lost people whose eternal life depends on that love. What more important work than this could we do? We dare not try to do this work in our own strength. We need to pray for all the help we can get in this intercessory work.

Our work of intercession is to bring a lost person and a loving Saviour together. It is acting on behalf of Jesus, to win men to Him, and on behalf of the sinner, to bring him to the Saviour.

When we intercede for lost people, we help them make peace with God through Christ. We tell them what Jesus has done for us and help them understand what the Word says to them about Jesus and themselves.

We intercede for lost people because we love them and we love the Saviour who loves them. We want to see two persons whom we love reconciled.

Personal evangelism is diplomacy. It is an effort to make peace between the sinner and the Saviour. It is negotiating a settlement in which the sinner gives up his old ways and surrenders his heart and life to Jesus in exchange for a new life.

With eternal consequences at hand, we should pray that God will help us in this important work. We need all the help we can get.

PATTERN FOR PRAYER
We Should Pray for Those Who
Have Already Come to Christ

"I pray for them: I pray not for the world, but for them which thou hast given me; for they are thine. And all mine are thine, and thine are mine; and I am glorified in them," Jesus prayed (John 17: 9, 10).

Jesus told His Father that He had made the Father's name known to men (v. 6) to show that He had been sent by the Father (v. 7), and that He had shared God's Word with men (v. 8).

The work for which Jesus had been sent (v. 4) was to bring eternal life to lost men (vs. 2, 3). This work was to bring glory to God and His Son, Jesus (vs. 1, 4, 5).

Now Jesus prays for His own, those who have become His followers. As we pray for the lost to come to Christ, so we also pray for the saved who have come to Him. This is intercessory prayer, too.

Christian brothers and sisters need our prayers more than we realize. When someone becomes a Christian, he is not suddenly relieved of all his problems. Instead, he has new problems to face as a Christian. But he has the Lord to help him. And he has us to pray for him. We are to bear one another's burdens "and so fulfil the law of Christ" (Galatians 6: 2).

If all Christians would intercede for one another in prayer, what a symphony of prayer would rise to the Lord for each of us. If Christians are weak in unity, it is because they are first weak in prayer for one another. Praying together is staying together in more than home and family relationships. This is true in all our Christian relationships.

"That they all may be one; as thou, Father, are in me, and I in thee, that they also may be one in us: that the world may believe that thou hast sent me," Jesus prayed (John 17: 21.)

Praying for one another encourages us to work for one another and live for one another and even die for one another. Jesus prayed that we who follow Him would be as united as He and His Father are united.

As those who marry are "one flesh" (Genesis 2: 24), so those who unite in Christ are one because they are united by "One Lord, one faith, one baptism, One God and Father of all, who is above all, and through all, and in you all" (Ephesians 4: 5, 6).

As all parts of the body work together in harmony, so all members of Christ's body should work together in unity. "For as the body is one, and hath many members, and all the members of that one body, being many, are one body: so also is Christ" (1 Corinthians 12: 12).

If one of us hurts, the others should hurt enough to pray and comfort. If one of us is hungry, the rest of us should be hungry enough to pray and share. If one of us is without, the rest of us should be concerned enough to pray and give.

Intercessory prayer is praying for others who know Christ. We all have special needs, even though we are Christians. Our greatest need is for each other's prayers.

We do not pray for our Christian friends to be taken away from their troubles. Instead, like Jesus, we pray for them to receive special help and strength to go through their troubles. Jesus prayed, "I pray not that thou shouldest take them out of the world, but that thou shouldest keep them from the evil [one]" (John 17: 15).

PATTERN FOR PRAYER
We Should Pray for Others
for the Glory of God

The recurrent theme running throughout Jesus' prayer is the glory of God and His Son Jesus.

"Glorify thy Son, that thy Son also may glorify thee" (v. 1).

"I have glorified thee on the earth" (v. 4).

"Glorify thou me with thine own self with the glory which I had with thee before the world was" (v. 5).

"I am glorified in them" (v. 10).

"And the glory thich thou gavest me I have given them" (v. 22).

"That they may behold my glory, which thou hast given me: for thou lovedst me before the foundation of the world" (v. 24).

The chief purpose of man is to glorify God. How much more true this is of the Christian. Our primary purpose is to bring honor to our Father and to our Saviour.

Every child is an ambassador for his family. Every child of God is an ambassador for Christ.

Every child wears his family name, to honor or dishonor it. Every child of God bears the name of Christ—Christian—to honor or dishonor that name above every name.

"Whether therefore ye eat, or drink, or whatsoever ye do, do all to the glory of God" (1 Corinthians 10: 31). This is our purpose in everything we do, even in praying for others.

Prayer reminders

When you intercede for others in prayer, remember to:

Pray that those who do not know God in Christ will come to know Him.

Pray that God will help you share your testimony and His Word so they will be won to Him.

Pray that God will help you to love the lost.

Pray for other Christians, that God will give them strength and wisdom to go through their problems.

Pray that you and other Christians may be one in Christ.

Pray that you may help others as you pray for them.

Pray that all that you do may bring glory to God, even what you do in behalf of others.

A prayer for those who suffer

*Jesus' Prayer
in Gethsemane*

Matthew 26: 36-45

Pathway to prayer

What led to Jesus' prayer in Gethsemane

When the Last Supper was over, Jesus and His disciples made their way by night through the streets of Jerusalem toward the eastern gate. They probably stopped at the Temple for awhile, where Jesus taught the disciples the things we now read in John 15 and 16, and prayed the prayer in John 17.

Leaving the Temple, they walked down through the Kidron Valley, then up into a quiet grove of olive trees on the western slope of the Mount of Olives.

The owner of this little garden was probably a friend of Jesus, and had invited Him to visit it whenever He wished. Now, on the night before His trial and crucifixion, Jesus sought the peaceful setting, away from the city streets, to talk with His Father in heaven alone.

The events of the next day weighed heavily on the Lord as He prayed. He knew that He would be mocked, beaten, insulted, spat upon, and rejected by those He wanted to save. He knew about His trial before Pilate and Herod. He knew also about the cross—and Calvary.

But the heaviest weight upon Him that night was not the physical suffering He would endure. It was the weight of sin. Jesus was about to take upon Himself the punishment for your sins and mine, and the sins of the world.

The weight of this punishment began to press upon Him there in the garden. The "cup" of suffering, as Jesus called it, was already tasting bitter. Jesus suffered. He hurt deeply. He was "exceeding sorrowful unto death" (Mark 14: 34).

When Jesus hurt, He did something about it. When he suffered, He took action.

With His closest earthly friends nearby, Jesus stepped apart a short distance to pray alone. There He shared His hurt and suffering with His Father in heaven.

Jesus' Prayer
in Gethsemane

Matthew 26:39, 42

O my Father, if it be possible, let this cup pass from me: nevertheless not as I will, but as thou wilt.

O my Father, if this cup may not pass away from me, except I drink it, thy will be done.

Patterns for prayer

from Jesus' prayer in Gethsemane

Suffering! What is it?

When we suffer, we hurt somewhere. A cut on the finger. An ache deep down inside where no medicine can reach. Or something much more complex than either of those.

Suffering is any one of many things. But everyone suffers at some time or other. None is spared. Do not mistake a smiling face as a sign that all is well. A bright coat of paint does not mean that all is at peace inside the house.

Suffering pushes rudely into already crowded places—ghettos, starving and overpopulated nations, and battlefields. It is cruel, oppressing the weak and helpless. It is savage, tearing at those who lack the personal and economic resources to resist.

Suffering visits some of us momentarily. Here today, gone tomorrow. But it establishes a permanent residence in hospitals, nursing homes, rehabilitation centers, and mental institutions.

No person is immune to suffering. No place is secure enough to lock it out. It may be starvation in the Orient or gout on Fifth Avenue. It may slip past the buzzer system of a high-rise or the double doors of a split-level suburban home.

Suffering is a child, bending over his dog that was run
over by the garbage truck. It is a white-haired grandmother,
waiting endlessly for children and grandchildren who are too
busy to come around much anymore.

Sometimes when we suffer, our body hurts. It may be as
elementary as a thorn under the fingernail or as complex as
terminal cancer for a blind amputee. Physical suffering is
constructed from raw materials such as pain, aches, nausea,
and shock.

Suffering may creep up on us, unannounced and unsuspected,
until we wake up to the reality of its presence. Or it may
come as dramatically as someone crashing into our car at
Fourth and Main five minutes after noon on a rainy day.

Some of our most painful suffering is more than physical.
We can hurt in our minds, where prescriptions become infinitely
complex.

We suffer mentally when bad news comes. "We regret to in-
form you," the telegram reads. Or the letter may begin, "Dear
John." Or the surgeon simply says, "I'm sorry, but . . . ."

Mental suffering may come from the absence of any news.
Wives of PW's may wait anxiously for some news—any news—
but it never comes. Suffering is wondering if you are a wife
or a widow, and if you will ever know the truth. Sometimes it
is wondering if you should even stop wondering.

Suffering is loss. It is Howard Hughes losing a million

when the Dow Jones average slips a few points. Or Jimmie
Washington losing some food stamps on the way to the grocer's.
It is a wife losing her wedding rings or a husband losing
his wallet and credit cards. It is a tiny child losing his
blanket or a big boy losing his favorite baseball card.

Suffering is waiting endlessly for something to happen,
but it never does. It is worrying endlessly for something
that never will be. It is endless fear for something unknown
and unlikely.

We suffer when we lose favor with the boss. We suffer when
marriage grows stale and ferments. We suffer when we're so
poor we don't know where to get the next penny, or when we're so
rich we don't know where to spend the next dollar.

When life becomes a pressure cooker and heats up our nerves
until they are raw, we suffer from nervous or emotional dis-
orders. Depression has become almost as prevalent as the common cold. Anxiety is as much a part of our way of life as
aspirin. It seems that just about all of us are nervous or
anxious about something.

Sometimes suffering is a very personal problem. Lest we
show people our weaknesses, we hide our suffering, even from
those who love us most. But secret suffering is dangerous.
It gnaws away at that vital possession called happiness.

Secret suffering magnifies insignificant threats into
phantom monsters which will never really materialize but

terrorize us anyway. It creates new worries and fears of what might have been, or could be, or may happen—but never materializes.

Suffering can be spiritual, too. Our desires and our conscience pinch from opposite directions, like the jaws of a nutcracker, and we are caught between.

Sin makes us suffer. It brings guilt and shame and tears. A suffering soul endures far more than a suffering mind or body.

Sometimes suffering is more than physical or mental or spiritual. Sometimes it is all three in a complex relationship. Physical suffering may bring about emotional suffering which may in turn cause spiritual suffering.

If we are looking for hope, let us look to Jesus. He suffered. No man has ever suffered more than He did. He suffered physically to the point of death. He suffered rejection from those whom He wanted to save. He suffered spiritually from our sins, as He took the punishment on Himself.

Jesus' prayer in Gethsemane gives help to those who suffer today. In His prayer, we find patterns for our prayers, patterns to help us face our suffering and overcome.

PATTERN FOR PRAYER
Prayer Puts Us in Touch With Someone Who
Understands Our Suffering and Gives Us Comfort

The suffering of the Saviour began before Calvary. Jesus
was suffering already "unto death" in Gethsemane. What did He
do when He suffered?

The Suffering Saviour fell down on His knees and talked
about His suffering with His Father in heaven. Jesus knew that
His Father was the only one who could understand what was in
His heart.

It's important to all of us to find someone who understands
when we hurt. A child runs to his mother or father when he hurts.
An understanding heart and a word of sympathy are like a
healing medicine. They cover the hurt and make us able to
bear it.

Prayer takes us to our Father in heaven. He understands all
about our suffering. He knows what is in our hearts and minds
and souls. And He knows what to do about these things. God's
Son knows about our suffering, too. He has gone through greater
suffering than we can ever face. The Holy Spirit understands.
That is why He is called The Comforter.

Jesus said, "And I will pray the Father, and he shall give
you another Comforter, that he may abide with you for ever"

(John 14: 16). The Father sent the Holy Spirit at the Son's request. We may have Someone nearby when we need help, Someone who can comfort us and counsel us.

Bearing our suffering alone is often more painful than the suffering itself. We bear our pain better when someone we love is there to console us. Fears are less frightening when a strong friend reassures us. Worry is less threatening when a friend shares his confidence with us.

What kind of counselor, or comforter, do we want when we hurt? We want someone who can truly sympathize because he has a heart of compassion. We want someone who can truly understand our hurt and our heart. We want someone who will listen to our problems. We want someone who will stay nearby while we suffer, going through that suffering with us.

The Lord is a Counselor and Comforter who meets every one of these requirements. Prayer puts us in touch with Him. Prayer opens the lines of communication with Someone who understands us better than our closest friends or relatives. Prayer establishes contact with Someone who knows suffering greater than any we will ever bear. Prayer puts a suffering person in the care and counsel of a loving God who wants to give unlimited help and comfort.

If the Lord is *your* Lord, then you should call upon Him to help you with your suffering. That's what Jesus did in Gethsemane.

PATTERN FOR PRAYER
Prayer Sends Us to Someone Who
Can Give Us Relief From Suffering

"O my Father, if it be possible, let this cup pass from
me," Jesus prayed (Matthew 26: 39). Even the Son of God looked
for some relief from suffering.

Jesus knew that His Father in heaven had the power to take
away all His suffering. If relief is right, God can and will
give it to those who love Him.

But taking away our suffering is not always what is best
for us. Nor is it always best for the Lord. There are reasons
why we hurt.

Jesus hurt in Gethsemane because He had an important work
to do. There was no way to do that work without suffering.
Suffering was intimately tied into His sacrifice for sin. To
relieve the suffering would be to cancel the work.

Sometimes we hurt for the same reason. We have an important
job to do for the Lord. To do that job effectively, we must
get hurt. Friends turn against us and that hurts. Serving God
doesn't pay much, and that hurts. Sometimes we face lonely
decisions where everyone seems to misunderstand us, and that
hurts. Those whom we seek to help often refuse our help, and
that hurts.

There are always reasons why we suffer. Sometimes we hurt because people misunderstand our good intentions. This is often the reason why Christians suffer when they try to do God's work. At other times, we hurt because we have done something wrong and the consequences are painful.

At times, we hurt because of no fault of our own. A car crashes into us and sends us to the hospital. We inherit a weakness through our family line. Or we are mistaken for someone else and hurt through mistaken identity.

What peculiar suffering do you have and why do you have it? Are you sure it would be best for you to be without it?

If we suffer for Christ, there are some very positive considerations. "If ye suffer for righteousness' sake, happy are ye," Peter wrote, "and be not afraid of their terror, neither be troubled" (1 Peter 3: 14).

But why should we be happy to suffer for Christ? "Because Christ also suffered for us, leaving us an example, that ye should follow his steps" (2: 21). Christ's suffering was "for us," for a positive purpose. "For it is better, if the will of God be so, that ye suffer for well doing, than for evil doing. For Christ also hath once suffered for sins, the just for the unjust, that he might bring us to God. . ." (3: 17, 18).

Suffering for a purpose is worth the pain. If we can help bring others to God, we should be willing to be hurt for that purpose.

Or if suffering will bring us nearer to God, then it has been worth it. Peter said, "That the trial of your faith, being much more precious than of gold that perisheth, though it be tried with fire, might be found unto praise and honour and glory at the appearing of Jesus Christ" (1: 7).

Suffering for Christ can bring honor and glory to our God, for we are following in Christ's steps. "If any man will come after me," Jesus said, "let him deny himself, and take up his cross, and follow me" (Matthew 16: 24). If we take up the cross, then we must suffer with Christ, but we do it for the glory of God, just as Jesus did.

"Yet if any man suffer as a Christian," Peter said, "let him not be ashamed; but let him glorify God on this behalf" (1 Peter 4: 16). If God is glorified through us, then we should rejoice. "Beloved, think it not strange concerning the fiery trial which is to try you, as though some strange thing happened unto you: But rejoice, inasmuch as ye are partakers of Christ's sufferings; that, when his glory shall be revealed, ye may be glad also with exceeding joy" (4: 12, 13).

Put your suffering in perspective before you expect God to remove it. If, by hurting, you can bring honor to God, can you expect God to remove it? When Jesus was willing to suffer the cross for you and me, can you ask to be excused from all suffering for Him?

This is perhaps the most critical test for suffering. Will it honor God in some way? If it will, should we ask God to take it away? Or should we ask for His will to be done?

PATTERN FOR PRAYER
Prayer Seeks God's Will
Concerning Our Suffering

"O my Father, if it be possible, let this cup pass from me: nevertheless not as I will, but as thou wilt," Jesus prayed.

If we are following Christ, we should also follow the pattern He set in His prayer. Not what we want, but what God wants should be our concern.

When Jesus gave The Lord's Prayer, He said that we should pattern our prayers after it. Part of The Lord's Prayer says, "Thy will be done in earth, as it is in heaven" (Matthew 6: 10).

Our requests should be conditioned by what God wants in our lives. Jesus said so in The Lord's Prayer. Jesus practiced in Gethsemane what He preached on the mount.

Doing God's will is a sign that we are His followers. "Not every one that saith unto me, Lord, Lord, shall enter into the kingdom of heaven; but he that doeth the will of my Father which is in heaven," Jesus said (7:21). Doing God's will shows others that we are true disciples. Jesus was saying that a true disciple is someone who not only calls on His name for salvation, but also follows the One who has saved him.

If Jesus has saved us from sin, then we should be following Him. If we follow Him, we should seek to do the will of God. Our prayers should seek God's will for all things, including our suffering.

"Not as I will, but as thou wilt," should be our prayer, as it was Jesus' prayer, in the hour of suffering. When you hurt, ask God what He wants to do about it. He may want you to endure it for His glory. Or He may want to help you find relief.

PATTERN FOR PRAYER
When You Pray Concerning Your Suffering,
Ask Your Christian Friends to Pray With You

"Tarry ye here, and watch with me," Jesus told His disciples (Matthew 26: 38). Jesus took His disciples to be near Him at the place of prayer. Those who were closest to Jesus went closest to Him as He prayed.

There is strength in companionship as we pray for God's answer to our suffering. When those who know and love the Lord draw near to us in our crisis experiences, we are the richer, for they undergird us as we pray for God's will to be done.

"Bear ye one another's burdens," we are told (Galatians 6: 2). This is part of our ministry as Christians, to help others through their suffering. You may do this for your fellow Christians. They may do it for you. Why? Because "ye are all one in Christ Jesus" (3: 28).

The disciples failed Jesus that night in Gethsemane. While He prayed, they fell asleep. They should have been praying with Him and for Him.

We need to watch that we do not fall asleep while our friends in Christ suffer in our presence. And while we suffer, we appreciate those who keep awake and pray with us.

"Tarry ye here, and watch with me."

"Bear ye one another's burdens."

Prayer reminders

When you pray and suffer, remember to:

Pray that God will comfort you in your suffering.

Pray that God will give you the strength to bear your suffering.

Pray that God will counsel you, so that you will know what you should do.

Pray that God will relieve your suffering, if it is His will to do so.

Pray that God will receive honor and glory from your suffering if He does not relieve you.

Pray that God's will may be done in whatever may happen in your life—in health or sickness, comfort or suffering.

Pray that God will give you peace of mind concerning the things you suffer.

Pray that God may use you as a source of strength to others who may be suffering, too.